Microwave
FISH AND SEAFOOD

© 1987 Illustrations and text: Colour Library Books Ltd.,
    Guildford, Surrey, England.
Text filmsetting by Focus Photoset Ltd., London, England.
All rights reserved.
Printed and bound in Barcelona, Spain by Cronión, S.A.
1987 edition published by Crescent Books, distributed by Crown Publishers, Inc.
ISBN 0 517 64076 7
h g f e d c b a

Microwave
FISH AND SEAFOOD

CRESCENT BOOKS
NEW YORK

4

CONTENTS

INTRODUCTION

A microwave oven is a fish kettle par excellence. In fact, many people prefer microwaved fish and shellfish to that cooked by conventional methods. Microwave cooking retains the natural moisture of food, something that is important in well-prepared fish. Fish and shellfish both require quick cooking, so the microwave oven really comes into its own.

Poaching is the fish cooking method that the microwave oven performs best. Use a shallow dish or a cooking bag and add white wine or water and lemon juice with peppercorns, onion slices and aromatic herbs, spices and vegetables. In a microwave oven all the flavor cooks into the fish, and low evaporation means plenty of liquid to make a good sauce.

A whole fish, such as a salmon or sea bass, can easily be poached providing the fish is not too large to allow it to turn freely. It is best to choose a fish no heavier than 2lbs in weight. Use a large cooking bag, securely tied, or a large, shallow dish covered with plastic wrap. Wrap the head and tail with foil to keep them from over-cooking and falling off. Cook 7-10 minutes on HIGH, or slightly longer on MEDIUM. The fish will continue to cook as it stands, so keep it covered while preparing sauces to accompany the fish. If you are not sure whether the fish is cooked, check close to the bone in an inconspicuous place. The flesh should be firm and opaque.

Even frying is possible, after a fashion, in a microwave oven. Dredge fish fillets or small whole fish with seasoned flour and preheat a browning dish. Fry in butter briefly on both sides to get a light brown, slightly crisp coating; a surprising result from a microwave oven.

Shellfish need careful cooking in a microwave oven or they toughen. Cook them no longer than 3 minutes on the highest setting or add them to a hot sauce at the last minute.

In the classification of fish there are four main categories: Flat fish, such as sole; Round fish, such as trout; Shellfish and Smoked fish, more popular in England and Europe than in the United States. Flat fish and round fish can be subdivided into oily fish, such as trout or salmon, and whitefish, such as sole or cod. But whatever fish you choose, your microwave oven will help you cook it to perfection.

FISH SOUPS

Spicy Clam Chowder

PREPARATION TIME: 15 minutes

MICROWAVE COOKING TIME:
12 minutes

SERVES: 4 people

2 tbsps butter or margarine
1 green pepper, diced
1 onion, finely sliced
1½ cups potatoes, diced
1lb can plum tomatoes
1lb can clams, liquid reserved
1 small chili pepper, finely chopped
Pinch cinnamon
Pinch nutmeg
Salt and pepper

**Melt the butter in a large bowl for
30 seconds on HIGH. Add the green
pepper, onion, potatoes and the
liquid from the clams. Cover the
bowl loosely and cook for 10 minutes
on HIGH or until the potatoes are
tender. Add the plum tomatoes,
clams, chili pepper, cinnamon,
nutmeg, and salt and pepper. Cook,
uncovered, for 2 minutes more on
HIGH. Serve immediately.**

Mariners' Chowder

PREPARATION TIME: 15 minutes

MICROWAVE COOKING TIME:
12 minutes

SERVES: 4 people

8oz whitefish
½ pint clams
½ pint mussels
8oz raw shrimp, peeled
3 tbsps butter
3 tbsps flour
1 onion, finely chopped

4 cups milk
¼ cup white wine
½ cup cream
1 bay leaf
2 tbsps chopped parsley
Salt and pepper

**This page: Mariners' Chowder
(top) and Spicy Clam Chowder
(bottom). Facing page: Cheese and
Clam Chowder (top) and Curried
Prawn Soup (bottom).**

Scrub the clams and mussels well. Discard any with broken or open shells. Put into a bowl with 2 tbsps water and cover loosely. Cook for 4 minutes on HIGH until the shells open. Discard any shellfish that do not open, remove the others from their opened shells, and set them aside. Combine the fish, shrimp and wine in a casserole and cook for 4 minutes, covered, on HIGH. Melt the butter for 30 seconds on HIGH in a large bowl. Add the onion and cook for 2 minutes on HIGH. Add the flour, milk, wine from the fish, salt and pepper. Cook for 5 minutes on HIGH, stirring frequently. Add the fish, shellfish, cream and parsley. Heat through for 1 minute on HIGH. Remove the bay leaf and serve.

Cheese and Clam Chowder

PREPARATION TIME: 15 minutes

MICROWAVE COOKING TIME: 13 minutes

SERVES: 4 people

2 1lb cans clams, liquid reserved
2 cups diced potatoes
1 onion, finely chopped
2 sticks celery, chopped
1 green pepper, chopped
3¼ cups milk
2 tbsps butter or margarine
2 tbsps flour
½ tsp dry mustard
Light cream as necessary
1 bay leaf
¼ tsp thyme
Dash Worcestershire sauce
2 tbsps chopped parsley
1 cup grated Colby cheese
Salt and pepper

Put the butter, onion, celery and pepper into a large bowl. Cover loosely and cook on HIGH for 2 minutes. Stir in the flour, mustard, milk and clam liquid. Blend well and add potatoes, thyme, salt and pepper. Put in the bay leaf, and cook on HIGH for 10 minutes, stirring occasionally. Remove the bay leaf and add the clams, cheese and

Worcestershire sauce. Heat for 2 minutes on MEDIUM to melt the cheese. Add light cream to thin the soup if it is too thick. Add the parsley to the soup and serve immediately.

Curried Prawn Soup

PREPARATION TIME: 10 minutes

MICROWAVE COOKING TIME: 8 minutes

SERVES: 4 people

3 tbsps butter or margarine
3 tbsps flour
2 tbsps curry powder
1 shallot, finely chopped
1 tsp mango chutney
1 tbsp lime juice
3 cups milk
1 cup fish or chicken stock
8oz cooked shrimp
Salt and pepper

GARNISH
Fresh coriander leaves or parsley
Plain yogurt

Melt the butter for 30 seconds on HIGH in a large bowl. Add the curry powder and the shallot and cook for 1 minute on HIGH. Stir in the flour, milk, stock, chutney, lime juice, salt and pepper. Cook for 5-6 minutes on HIGH until thickened. Add the shrimp and cook for 30 seconds on HIGH. Serve garnished with coriander and yogurt.

Lobster Bisque

PREPARATION TIME: 15 minutes

MICROWAVE COOKING TIME: 9 minutes

SERVES: 4 people

1 large lobster tail, uncooked
4 tbsps butter or margarine
4 tbsps flour
1 shallot, finely chopped
2 cups milk
1 cup cream
1 cup fish or chicken stock
1 bay leaf
Celery salt

Pepper
Cayenne pepper
4 tbsps dry sherry

Remove the lobster tail meat from the shell. Break the shell into small pieces. Melt the butter in a small bowl for 30 seconds on HIGH. Put in the shell pieces and the shallot and cook for 1 minute on HIGH or until the shell turns red. Strain the butter into a large, clean bowl. Cut the lobster meat into small pieces and add to the butter. Cook for 1-2 minutes on HIGH. Remove the meat and set it aside. Stir the flour, celery salt and Cayenne pepper into the butter. Add the bay leaf, milk and stock. Cook for 5-6 minutes on HIGH to thicken. Add the sherry and the lobster meat and heat through for 1 minute on HIGH. Remove the bay leaf and swirl the cream through the soup. Serve immediately.

Smoked Salmon Cream Soup

PREPARATION TIME: 15 minutes

MICROWAVE COOKING TIME: 7-8 minutes

SERVES: 4 people

8oz whitefish, cut into 1" chunks
8oz smoked salmon, cut into 1" pieces
3 tbsps butter or margarine
2 tbsps flour
½ cup white wine
3 cups milk
½ cup light cream
Pepper

GARNISH
Sour cream
Chopped chives

Cook the whitefish and wine for 2 minutes on HIGH. Melt the butter for 30 seconds on HIGH. Stir in the flour and milk, the whitefish and its

Facing page: Smoked Salmon Cream Soup (top) and Lobster Bisque (bottom).

cooking liquid. Cook for 5-6 minutes, stirring frequently, until thick. Add pepper, smoked salmon and cream. Work in a food processor until smooth. Re-heat for 1 minute on HIGH and add salt to taste. Garnish each serving with a spoonful of sour cream and a sprinkling of chopped chives.

Creamy Crab Soup

PREPARATION TIME: 15 minutes

MICROWAVE COOKING TIME: 9 minutes

SERVES: 4 people

1lb crabmeat, fresh or frozen
4 tbsps butter or margarine
4 tbsps flour
1 shallot, finely chopped
3 cups milk
½ cup cream
½ cup stock
2 tbsps white wine
Cayenne pepper
Salt and pepper

GARNISH
Chopped chives

Put the butter and shallot into a casserole. Cover and cook for 3 minutes on HIGH, stirring occasionally. Stir in the flour, milk, stock, Cayenne pepper, salt and pepper. Cook for 5 minutes on HIGH, stirring frequently until thickened. Add the crabmeat, cream and wine, and cook for a further 1 minute on HIGH. Serve garnished with chopped chives.

Shrimp and Chinese Mushroom Soup

PREPARATION TIME: 15 minutes

MICROWAVE COOKING TIME: 9 minutes

SERVES: 4 people

4oz fine Chinese egg noodles
8 dried Chinese mushrooms
¾ cup shrimp, cooked and peeled

1 small can water chestnuts, sliced
1 small can bamboo shoots, sliced
Bunch green onions, sliced diagonally
¼ lb peapods, trimmed
1 tbsp light soy sauce
2 tbsps dry sherry
1 tsp sesame seed oil
1 tbsp cornstarch
4 cups chicken or fish stock
Salt and pepper

Put the mushrooms into a small bowl with enough water to cover. Cook on HIGH for 2 minutes and leave to stand. Mix the cornstarch with 2 tbsps stock, and set aside. Combine the remaining stock, peapods and noodles. Cook for 2 minutes on HIGH. Add the cornstarch mixture and all the remaining ingredients, and cook for a further 5 minutes on HIGH. Serve immediately.

Oyster and Watercress Soup

PREPARATION TIME: 15 minutes

MICROWAVE COOKING TIME: 13 minutes

SERVES: 4 people

1lb can oysters
Bunch watercress

3 cups diced potatoes
1½ cups liquid reserved from oysters
1½ cups light cream
1 cup milk
1 shallot, finely chopped
3 tbsps butter or margarine
Nutmeg
Lemon juice
Salt and pepper

Drain the oysters and add water to the liquid, if necessary, to measure 1½ cups. Melt the butter in a large bowl for 30 seconds on HIGH. Add the potatoes, shallot, stock, nutmeg, salt and pepper. Cover loosely and cook on HIGH for 10 minutes, or until the potatoes are tender. Add the milk and half the oysters. Chop the watercress, reserving 4 sprigs for garnish, and add to the bowl. Cook, uncovered, for 2 minutes on HIGH. Put into a food processor and purée until smooth. Return to the bowl and add the remaining oysters, cream and lemon juice. Heat through for 1 minute on HIGH. Serve garnished with the reserved watercress.

This page: Shrimp and Chinese Mushroom Soup. Facing page: Creamy Crab Soup (top) and Oyster and Watercress Soup (bottom).

APPETIZERS AND FIRST COURSES

Florentine Shrimp Tarts

PREPARATION TIME: 20 minutes

MICROWAVE COOKING TIME:
9-10 minutes

SERVES: 4 people

4 slices wholewheat bread
¼ cup butter, melted
1½ lbs fresh spinach, washed (or ¾ lb
    frozen spinach, thawed)
2 tbsps heavy cream
Nutmeg, grated
8 large, unpeeled shrimp, cooked

SAUCE
½ cup butter
3 egg yolks
1 tbsp white wine vinegar
Cayenne pepper
Salt and pepper

GARNISH
Fresh chives or chervil

Cut the crusts off the bread and roll out each slice very thinly. Cut out a 4″ round from each slice and brush both sides with melted butter. Mold into 4 individual pie or flan pans, preferably false-bottomed. Cook on HIGH for 2-3 minutes until crisp. Cook the fresh spinach in a large bowl, loosely covered, for 2 minutes on HIGH with 2 tbsps water. Drain the spinach well, squeezing out all the moisture whether using fresh or frozen spinach. Heat 1 tbsp of the remaining butter in a large bowl for 1 minute on HIGH. Toss in the spinach, salt, pepper and nutmeg. Stir in the cream and set aside. Peel the shrimp carefully and set aside. Prepare the sauce by melting the butter in a small, deep bowl for 1 minute on HIGH. Mix the egg yolks, salt, pepper, Cayenne pepper and vinegar together, and pour into the hot butter, beating constantly. Have a bowl of ice water ready. Cook the sauce for 30 seconds on HIGH, then beat well. Repeat until the sauce thickens, which takes about 2 minutes. Put the sauce bowl immediately into ice water to stop the cooking. Remove and set aside. Put the spinach into the bread shells and top with the shrimp. Heat through for 30 seconds on HIGH. Pour over the sauce and heat for 20 seconds on MEDIUM. Serve garnished with chives or chervil.

This page: Florentine Shrimp Tarts. Facing page: Shrimp Kebabs Vera Cruz.

Shrimp Kebabs Vera Cruz

PREPARATION TIME: 15 minutes

MICROWAVE COOKING TIME:
4 minutes

SERVES: 4 people

2 dozen large shrimp, peeled and
*   uncooked*
4oz chorizo or pepperoni, cut into
*   ¼" slices.*
1 large green pepper
2 tbsps olive oil
1 ripe avocado
2 tomatoes, peeled, seeded and finely
*   chopped*
1 clove garlic, crushed
Cayenne pepper
Lemon juice
Salt and pepper

Alternate the shrimp, sausage and green pepper on wooden skewers. Brush with oil. Peel and mash the avocado with the garlic, lemon juice, Cayenne pepper, and salt and pepper. Stir in the tomatoes. Cook the kebabs on a roasting rack for 3 minutes on HIGH, and heat the sauce for 30 seconds on HIGH. Serve immediately.

Layered Seafood Terrine

PREPARATION TIME: 20 minutes

MICROWAVE COOKING TIME:
12 minutes, plus 5 minutes standing time

SERVES: 4 people

12oz whitefish, skinned and cut into
*   chunks*
3oz crabmeat
3oz lobster
¼ cup cream cheese
2 eggs
1 cup fresh white breadcrumbs
2 tbsps heavy cream
2 tbsps white wine
Chopped parsley
Cayenne pepper
Salt and pepper

BERNAISE SAUCE
3 egg yolks
½ cup butter
1 tbsp chopped mixed herbs
1 tbsp white wine vinegar
Salt and pepper

Combine the eggs, whitefish, cheese, cream, crumbs, wine, salt and pepper in a food processor and work until smooth. Divide the mixture into thirds. Mix the crab and parsley into one third, the lobster and Cayenne pepper into another third, and leave the remaining third plain. Line a 1lb glass loaf dish with wax paper, and layer in the crabmeat, whitefish and lobster mixtures. Cover well with plastic wrap and cook for 10 minutes on MEDIUM. Put a small dish of water into the oven with the terrine to keep it moist. Allow to stand for 5 minutes while preparing the sauce. Beat the egg yolks, vinegar, herbs and salt and pepper together. Melt the butter for 1 minute on HIGH in a small, deep bowl. Beat the egg yolks into the butter. Have a bowl of ice water ready. Cook the sauce ingredients for 15 seconds on HIGH and then stir well. Repeat the process until the sauce thickens, which takes about 2 minutes. Put the sauce immediately into the bowl of ice water to stop the cooking. Slice the terrine and serve with the Bernaise Sauce.

Crab-Stuffed Pea Pods

PREPARATION TIME: 20 minutes

MICROWAVE COOKING TIME:
2 minutes

SERVES: 4 people

1lb pea pods

FILLING
½ cup crabmeat
1 package garlic-and-herb soft cheese
2 tbsps white wine
1 tbsp milk or light cream

Mix the filling ingredients together, breaking up the crabmeat well. Wash the pea pods and carefully split down one side of each to form pockets. Blanch for 1 minute on HIGH with 4 tbsps water in a loosely-covered bowl. Rinse under cold water and dry well. Carefully open each pocket. Put the filling into a pastry bag fitted with a ½" plain tube and pipe the filling into the pea pods. Arrange on individual dishes and heat for 30 seconds on HIGH. Serve with lemon slices or wedges.

Herbed Fish Pâté with Lemon-Orange Hollandaise Sauce

PREPARATION TIME: 20 minutes

MICROWAVE COOKING TIME:
12 minutes, plus 5 minutes standing time

SERVES: 4 people

1lb whitefish (sole, flounder or cod)
4oz Parma ham, thinly sliced
4 tbsps chopped mixed herbs
1 cup fresh white breadcrumbs
2 eggs
¼ cup low-fat soft cheese, or Ricotta
*   cheese*
2 tbsps heavy cream
Salt and pepper

HOLLANDAISE SAUCE
3 egg yolks
½ cup butter
1 tbsp lemon juice
1 tbsp orange juice and rind
Salt and pepper

Line a 1lb glass loaf dish with the slices of Parma ham. Skin and cut the fish into chunks. Combine all the remaining pâté ingredients in a food processor and work until smooth. Spoon onto the ham and smooth out. Fold the ends of the ham over the pâté mixture. Cover well with plastic wrap and cook on MEDIUM for 10 minutes, or until just firm. Put a small dish of water into the microwave oven with the pâté to keep it moist. Leave to stand for 5 minutes before turning out and slicing for serving. To prepare the

Facing page: Layered Seafood Terrine (top) and Herbed Fish Pâté with Lemon-Orange Hollandaise Sauce.

½ tsp grated horseradish
1 tbsp snipped chives or chopped green
  onion
1 tbsp sesame seeds
1 tbsp poppy seeds
2 tbsps butter, melted
Salt and pepper

Scrub, but do not peel, the potatoes,
Pierce them several times with a fork.
Mix the cheese, crab, horseradish,
chives and salt and pepper together.
Cook the potatoes with enough
water to barely cover for 4 minutes
on HIGH. When cooked, slice ½″ off
the top of each potato and reserve.
Spoon 1 tsp of the crab filling into
the bottom portion of the potatoes.
Top with the lids and put the filled
potatoes onto a plate. Pour some of
the melted butter over each potato
and sprinkle on a mixture of the
sesame and poppy seeds. Heat for 30
seconds on HIGH.

Scallops with Red and Gold Sauces

PREPARATION TIME: 15 minutes

MICROWAVE COOKING TIME:
12 minutes

SERVES: 4 people

2lb fresh scallops
½ lb fresh bean sprouts
1 large, ripe avocado
4 tbsps lime juice
2 sweet red peppers
2 yellow peppers
1 tbsp grated ginger
1 cup water
2 tbsps desiccated coconut
1 tbsp ground almonds
Pinch Cayenne pepper
Salt and pepper

Put scallops in a casserole with 4
tbsps water and 1½ tsps lime juice.
Cover loosely and cook on HIGH

sauce, melt the butter in a small glass
bowl for 1 minute on HIGH. Beat the
egg yolks with the salt, pepper, lemon
juice, orange juice and rind. Mix the
egg yolks with the butter, stirring
constantly. Have a bowl of ice water
ready. Cook the sauce for 15 seconds
on HIGH. Stir well, and repeat the
process until the sauce thickens,
which takes about 2 minutes. Put the
sauce immediately into the bowl of
ice water to stop the cooking. Serve
with the pâté.

Crab-Stuffed New Potatoes

PREPARATION TIME: 15 minutes

MICROWAVE COOKING TIME:
5 minutes

SERVES: 4 people with
3 potatoes each

12 small new potatoes, uniform in size
½ cup cream or low-fat soft cheese
½ cup crabmeat

**This page: Scallops with Red and
Gold Sauces. Facing page: Crab-
Stuffed Pea Pods (top) and Crab-
Stuffed New Potatoes (bottom).**

for 1 minute. Turn the scallops over after 30 seconds. Slice the scallops in half through the middle if they are large. Slice the red and yellow peppers, and put them into separate bowls with half the remaining lime juice and water in each. Cover with pierced plastic wrap and cook each for 5 minutes on HIGH, or until the peppers are very soft. Put the yellow peppers and liquid into a food processor with the ginger and salt and pepper, and work to a smooth purée. Strain if necessary. Work the red peppers in the same way but with the almonds, coconut, Cayenne pepper, and salt and pepper. Peel and slice the avocado thinly. Divide the red sauce evenly on 4 salad plates, covering one side, and put the equivalent gold sauce on the other side of each plate. Arrange the scallops, bean sprouts and avocado slices on top of the sauce to serve.

Oysters Florentine

PREPARATION TIME: 15 minutes

MICROWAVE COOKING TIME:
5 minutes

SERVES: 4 people

2 dozen oysters on the half shell
1lb spinach, washed, or ½ lb frozen
*   spinach, thawed*
¼ cup heavy cream
Nutmeg
Salt and pepper

SAUCE
3 egg yolks
½ cup butter
1 shallot, finely chopped
2 tbsps lemon juice mixed with Tabasco

GARNISH
Lemon slices

Cook the spinach with 1 tbsp water for 1 minute on HIGH in a large bowl loosely covered. Drain well and season with salt and pepper. Add the nutmeg and cream. Put a spoonful of spinach on top of each oyster. Melt the butter on HIGH for 1 minute with the shallot. Mix the egg yolks with lemon juice and Tabasco, and

pour into the hot butter, beating constantly. Have a bowl of ice water ready. Cook for 30 seconds on HIGH and stir. Repeat the process until the sauce thickens (about 2 minutes). Put the sauce bowl immediately into ice water to stop the cooking. Remove and set aside. Top each oyster with a spoonful of the sauce and heat through for 30 seconds on MEDIUM. Garnish with lemon slices.

NOTE: Oysters can be opened easily in microwave ovens. Clean the shells well, and leave to soak in clean water for 2 hours. Cook for 45 seconds on

HIGH, insert a knife near the hinge and pry open.

Crab-Stuffed Avocados

PREPARATION TIME: 15 minutes

MICROWAVE COOKING TIME:
3 minutes

SERVES: 4 people

**This page: Crab-Stuffed
Artichoke (top) and Crab-Stuffed
Avocados (bottom). Facing page:
Oysters Florentine.**

2 ripe avocados, cut in half and stones
    removed
½ lb crabmeat
1 green pepper, diced
2 sticks celery, diced
2 green onions, chopped
1 cup prepared mayonnaise
2 tbsps heavy cream
1 tbsp chili sauce
Lemon juice
Salt and pepper
Paprika

Scoop out some of the avocado and chop the flesh roughly. Sprinkle the shell and the chopped flesh with lemon juice. Put the pepper, celery and onion into a small bowl with 2 tbsps water. Cover loosely and cook for 2 minutes on HIGH to soften. Drain away the water and mix in the crab, mayonnaise, cream, chili sauce and salt and pepper. Carefully fold in the reserved avocado flesh. Pile into the avocado shells and sprinkle with paprika. Cook for 1 minute on HIGH, with the narrow end of the avocados pointing to the middle of the dish. Serve immediately.

Stuffed Artichokes

PREPARATION TIME: 20 minutes

MICROWAVE COOKING TIME:
17-19 minutes

SERVES: 4 people

4 globe artichokes
1 bay leaf
1 slice lemon

FILLING
1 cup crabmeat, flaked
3 tbsps butter
3 tbsps flour
2 tbsps Dijon mustard
2 tbsps snipped chives
1 cup milk
½ cup white wine
Salt and pepper

Trim the points of the artichoke leaves and cut the stems so that the artichokes will sit upright. Put them into a large, deep bowl with enough water to barely cover. Add the bay

leaf and lemon slice. Cook for 15 minutes on HIGH. Drain upside-down. Melt the butter in a small, deep bowl for 30 seconds on HIGH. Stir in the flour, milk, wine, salt and pepper. Cook for 2-3 minutes on HIGH. Stir every 30 seconds. Add the mustard and chives. Add the crabmeat and keep warm. Remove the center leaves of the artichoke and carefully lift away the thistle-like choke with a teaspoon. Pour in the crabmeat filling and serve hot.

Lobster Julienne

PREPARATION TIME: 20 minutes

MICROWAVE COOKING TIME:
9-10 minutes

SERVES: 4 people

1 large lobster tail, uncooked
2 tbsps butter or margarine
2 carrots, cut in thin, 2" strips
1 leek, cut in thin, 2" strips
2 zucchini, cut into 2" strips
2 sticks celery, cut in 2" strips
8 mushrooms, thinly sliced
½ cup white wine
2 tbsps cornstarch
1 tbsp lemon juice
½ cup whole milk yogurt
2 tsps crushed tarragon
Salt and pepper

GARNISH
Chopped parsley

Melt half the butter for 30 seconds on HIGH in a small casserole. Add the carrot and celery and 1 tbsp white wine. Cover and cook for 1 minute on HIGH. Add the zucchini, leek and mushrooms. Cover the casserole and cook for 2 minutes on HIGH and set aside. Heat a browning dish for 3 minutes on HIGH. Remove the lobster tail meat from the shell and cut into ½" slices. Drop the remaining butter into the browning dish and add the lobster meat. Cook for 1 minute on HIGH. Remove the lobster and mix with the vegetables. Mix the cornstarch with the lemon juice, remaining wine, tarragon, salt and pepper. Cook for 1-2 minutes on

HIGH until thickened. Stir in the yogurt and heat through for 30 seconds on HIGH. Toss the lobster and vegetables with the sauce and serve immediately, garnished with chopped parsley.

Chinese Shrimp Parcels

PREPARATION TIME: 20 minutes

MICROWAVE COOKING TIME:
6-7 minutes

SERVES: 4 people

1 head Chinese cabbage

FILLING
½ cup cashew nuts
4 green onions, chopped
8oz cooked shrimp
½ cup chopped water chestnuts
2 cups bean sprouts
8 dried Chinese mushrooms, soaked
1 red pepper, chopped
1 tbsp cornstarch
2 tbsps white wine

SWEET AND SOUR MUSTARD SAUCE
2 tbsps honey
2 tbsps white wine vinegar
4 tbsps Dijon mustard
1 tbsp cornstarch
½ cup white wine
½ cup water
2 tbsps soy sauce

Separate 8 of the largest and best-looking leaves of the Chinese cabbage. Trim down their spines to make them easier to roll up. Put them into a large bowl with 2 tbsps water. Cover the bowl loosely and cook the leaves for 30 seconds on HIGH to soften slightly. Slice the mushrooms and roughly chop the cashews, then mix with the remaining filling ingredients. Put 2 leaves together, slightly overlapping, and

Facing page: Lobster Julienne (top) and South Seas Tidbits (bottom).

divide the filling equally among all the leaves. Tuck the sides of the leaves around the filling and roll up. Repeat with the remaining leaves and filling. Put folded edge down in a large casserole with 2 tbsps water. Cover loosely and cook for 3 minutes on HIGH. Set aside while preparing the sauce. Mix all the sauce ingredients together and cook for 2-3 minutes on HIGH. Stir every 30 seconds until the sauce thickens. Set aside.

Above: Chinese Shrimp Parcels (top) and Steamed Crabmeat Wontons (bottom).

South Seas Tidbits

PREPARATION TIME: 15 minutes

MICROWAVE COOKING TIME:
5-6 minutes

SERVES: 4 people

1lb can pineapple chunks, juice reserved
1 papaya, peeled and cut into 1" chunks
8oz raw shrimp, peeled
8oz scallops

SAUCE
2 tbsps brown sugar
1 tbsp cornstarch
1 tbsp soy sauce
1 tbsp cider vinegar
Large pinch ground ginger
2 tbsps desiccated coconut
2 green onions, chopped

Mix all the sauce ingredients, except the coconut, together with ¾ cup reserved pineapple juice. Cook for 2-3 minutes on HIGH, stirring until thickened. Add the shrimp and scallops and cook for a further 2 minutes on HIGH. Add the pineapple, papaya and coconut and cook for a further 30 seconds on HIGH. Serve as an appetizer.

Steamed Crabmeat Wontons

PREPARATION TIME: 20 minutes

MICROWAVE COOKING TIME:
5 minutes for wontons; 2-3 minutes per sauce

SERVES: 4 people

30 fresh wonton skins

FILLING
12oz cooked crabmeat, fresh or frozen
2 green onions, chopped
6 water chestnuts, chopped
1 tbsp grated fresh ginger root
1 tbsp sherry or white wine
1 tbsp sesame seed oil
1 egg
Salt and pepper

SWEET AND SOUR SAUCE
¾ cup orange juice
2 tbsps soy sauce
1½ tbsps brown sugar
1½ tbsps cider vinegar
2 tsps cornstarch
1½ tbsps ketchup

HOT MUSTARD SAUCE
4 tbsps dry mustard
1½ tsps cornstarch
4 tbsps white wine vinegar
½ cup water
¼ cup honey
Salt

Mix all the filling ingredients together. Just before filling each skin, brush both sides with water. Put a rounded tsp of the filling in the center of each skin and pinch the edges together, leaving some of the filling showing. Lightly grease a plate or microwave baking sheet and place the wontons on it. Pour 2 tbsps water over the wontons. Cover them loosely with plastic wrap and cook for 1 minute on HIGH. Lower the setting to LOW and cook for 4 further minutes. Cook in two batches. Brush the wontons several times with water while cooking. Serve with one or both of the sauces. For the sweet and sour sauce, mix the sauce ingredients and cook in a small, deep bowl, uncovered, for 2-3 minutes on HIGH. Stir every 30 seconds until the sauce has thickened. For the hot mustard sauce, mix the mustard and cornstarch together. Beat in the water, vinegar and honey gradually until the sauce is smooth. Add salt and cook, uncovered, in a small, deep bowl for 2-3 minutes on HIGH. Stir every 30 seconds until thickened.

Coriander Mussels

PREPARATION TIME: 15 minutes

MICROWAVE COOKING TIME: 4-6 minutes

SERVES: 4 people

1 quart mussels
2 shallots, finely chopped
1 cup white wine
1 tbsp coriander seeds, crushed
1 tbsp butter
1 tbsp flour
½ cup cream
1 tbsp chopped coriander
1 tbsp chopped parsley
Salt and pepper

Scrub the mussels well and discard

any with broken or open shells. Put the mussels into a large bowl with the shallots, wine and coriander seeds. Cook for 1-2 minutes on HIGH, stirring every 30 seconds, until shells open. Discard any mussels that do not open. Strain the cooking liquid. Melt the butter in a small, deep bowl for 30 seconds on HIGH. Stir in the flour, cream, strained liquid, and salt and pepper. Cook for 2-3 minutes on HIGH until thickened, stirring every 30 seconds. Add the chopped coriander and parsley. Divide the mussels into

Above: Coriander Mussels.

individual bowls and pour over the sauce to serve.

Brandied Shrimp

PREPARATION TIME: 10 minutes

MICROWAVE COOKING TIME: 4 minutes

SERVES: 4 people

2¼ lbs uncooked shrimp, peeled
1½ cups dry breadcrumbs
4 tbsps brandy

½ cup butter
2 shallots, chopped
4 tbsps chopped parsley
Paprika
Salt and pepper

GARNISH
4 lemon wedges

Mix the shallot, salt, pepper, parsley and shrimp together and divide between 4 small baking dishes. Pour brandy over each dish and cook for 30 seconds on HIGH. Heat a browning dish for 5 minutes on HIGH. Drop in the butter and cook for a further 30 seconds on HIGH. Stir in the breadcrumbs and cook for 1-2 minutes to brown. Spoon the breadcrumbs over the shrimp and sprinkle on the paprika. Cook for 1 minute on HIGH or until the shrimp are cooked. Serve with lemon wedges.

Marinated Herring with Tomatoes

PREPARATION TIME: 20 minutes

MICROWAVE COOKING TIME:
5-7 minutes

SERVES: 4 people

8 herring fillets

MARINADE
2 onions, finely chopped
¾ cup red wine vinegar
¼ cup water
¼ cup sugar
6 black peppercorns
2 whole allspice berries

SAUCE
4 tomatoes, peeled, seeded and cut into
   thin strips
2 tbsps tomato paste
2 tbsps snipped chives
⅓ cup vegetable oil
¼ cup reserved marinade
Salt and pepper

Combine the marinade ingredients and cook, uncovered, for 5-7 minutes on HIGH until rapidly boiling. Allow to cool slightly, and pour over the fish fillets. Leave the fish to cool

completely in the marinade. Mix the oil and strained reserved marinade together with the tomato paste, chives, salt and pepper. Pour over the herring and top with the tomato strips to serve.

Smoky Cheese and Shrimp Dip

PREPARATION TIME: 15 minutes

MICROWAVE COOKING TIME:
5 minutes

SERVES: 4 people

1½ cups shredded Cheddar cheese

This page: Smoky Cheese and Shrimp Dip. Facing page: Brandied Shrimp (top) and Marinated Herring with Tomatoes (bottom).

1 cup shredded smoked or smoky cheese
1 tbsp butter
1 shallot, finely chopped
½ cup shrimp, chopped
¾ cup light cream
½ oz flour
Salt and pepper
Raw vegetables

Melt the butter in a small, deep bowl for 30 seconds on HIGH. Add the shallot and cook for 1 minute on HIGH to soften. Toss the cheese and

flour together and add to the bowl with the shallot. Stir in the cream, salt and pepper. Cook for 4 minutes on MEDIUM or until the cheese has melted. Stir the mixture twice while cooking. Serve hot with vegetable crudités for dipping.

Herring in Mustard Dill Sauce

PREPARATION TIME: 20 minutes

MICROWAVE COOKING TIME: 7-9 minutes

SERVES: 4 people

4 herring fillets, cut in chunks

MARINADE
2 onions, finely chopped
¾ cup white wine vinegar
¼ cup water
¼ cup sugar
4 sprigs fresh dill
1 tbsp dried dill
6 black peppercorns
2 whole allspice berries

SAUCE
1 tbsp flour
2 tbsps mustard
1 tbsp chopped dill
¼ cup sour cream

Combine the marinade ingredients and cook, uncovered, for 5-7 minutes until rapidly boiling. Allow to cool slightly, and pour over the fish. Leave the fish to cool in the marinade. Strain the marinade and beat gradually into the flour. Add the mustard and cook for 2 minutes on HIGH, stirring every 30 seconds until thickened. Mix with the chopped dill, and chill. Mix in the sour cream and herring. Serve as an appetizer, or on a bed of lettuce as a first course.

Oysters Romanoff

PREPARATION TIME: 10 minutes

MICROWAVE COOKING TIME: 1 minute

SERVES: 4 people

2 dozen oysters on the half shell
1½ tbsps snipped chives
1 cup sour cream
1 jar red lumpfish or salmon caviar
Lemon juice
Salt and pepper

Put a drop of lemon juice on each oyster. Mix the chives and cream together with salt and pepper. Put a spoonful of the mixture on top of each oyster. Heat through for 1 minute on HIGH on a large plate. Heat in 2 batches if necessary. Put a spoonful of the caviar on each oyster before serving. Serve with lemon wedges and watercress.

This page: Pickled Mussels (top) and Herring in Mustard Dill Sauce (bottom). Facing page: Oysters Romanoff.

Pickled Mussels

PREPARATION TIME: 15 minutes

MICROWAVE COOKING TIME: 6 minutes

SERVES: 4 people

1 quart mussels
½ cup white wine
½ cup white wine vinegar

2 tbsps sugar
1 tbsp mustard seed
1 cinnamon stick
4 whole allspice berries
4 black peppercorns
4 whole cloves
2 shallots, finely chopped
Salt and pepper

Scrub the mussels well and discard any with broken or open shells. Put the mussels into a large bowl with 2 tbsps water. Cook on HIGH for 45-50 seconds, until the shells open, stirring twice. Discard any mussels that do not open. Combine the remaining ingredients, and cook for 5 minutes on HIGH or until boiling. Allow to cool slightly. Remove the mussels from their shells and combine with the pickling mixture. Leave to cool and then refrigerate. Keep no longer than 2 days.

Salmon Terrine

PREPARATION TIME: 15 minutes

MICROWAVE COOKING TIME:
10 minutes

SERVES: 4 people

1lb salmon
2 eggs
1 cup fresh white breadcrumbs
¼ cup cream cheese
2 tbsps heavy cream
Salt and pepper

DRESSING
1 cucumber, grated
1 cup sour cream
½ cup prepared mayonnaise
2 tbsps chopped dill
Salt and pepper

GARNISH
Red lumpfish caviar

Skin the salmon and cut into chunks. Combine with the remaining terrine ingredients in a food processor and work until smooth. Line the bottom of a 1lb glass loaf dish with waxed paper. Fill with the salmon mixture and smooth out. Cover well with plastic wrap and cook for 10 minutes

on MEDIUM, with a small dish of water to keep it moist. Allow to cool and then chill well. Turn out and cut into slices. Mix all the dressing ingredients together and serve with the terrine. Garnish with the lumpfish caviar.

Smoked Oyster Pâté

PREPARATION TIME: 15 minutes

MICROWAVE COOKING TIME:
10 minutes, plus 5 minutes standing time

SERVES: 4 people

1 can smoked oysters
1lb whitefish
1 cup fresh white breadcrumbs
Butter
2 eggs
¼ cup cream cheese
2 tbsps cream
1 tbsp chopped parsley
2 tsps Worcestershire sauce
1 tbsp lemon juice
Salt and pepper

Roughly chop the smoked oysters. Combine the remaining ingredients in a food processor and work until smooth. Fold in the oysters. Line the bottom of a 1lb glass loaf dish with waxed paper. Spoon in the pâté mixture and smooth out. Cover well with plastic wrap and cook for 10 minutes on MEDIUM. Put a small dish of water into the oven with the pâté to keep it moist. Leave to stand for 5 minutes, then chill before serving. Serve with buttered toast.

Paprika Shrimp

PREPARATION TIME: 15 minutes

MICROWAVE COOKING TIME:
10 minutes

SERVES: 4 people

2lbs raw shrimp, peeled
¼ cup butter or margarine
1 tbsp paprika
2 chopped shallots
1 red pepper, thinly sliced

2 tbsps chopped parsley
1½ cups sour cream
1 tbsp lemon juice
Salt and pepper

TOPPING
¼ cup butter or margarine
½ cup breadcrumbs

Heat a browning dish for 5 minutes on HIGH. Melt the butter for the topping and stir in the breadcrumbs. Cook on HIGH for 2 minutes, stirring every 30 seconds. Set aside. Melt the remaining butter in a large casserole for 30 seconds on HIGH. Add the paprika, shallot and sliced pepper. Cook for 2 minutes on HIGH, stirring frequently. Add the shrimp, lemon juice, salt and pepper, and continue cooking for 2 minutes more on HIGH. Stir in the sour cream. Put into individual serving dishes and sprinkle over the browned crumbs. Cook for 30 seconds on MEDIUM to heat through, and serve with hot rolls or French bread.

Calamares España

PREPARATION TIME: 20 minutes

MICROWAVE COOKING TIME:
8 minutes

SERVES: 4 people

2 medium-sized squid
2 tbsps olive oil
2 tbsps flour flour
1 clove garlic, finely chopped
2 cups canned plum tomatoes
1 chili pepper, finely chopped
Grated rind and juice of 1 orange
½ cup white wine
1 tbsp tomato paste
1 tsp oregano
1 tsp basil
1 bay leaf
Salt and pepper

GARNISH
Fresh coriander leaves

Facing page: Smoked Oyster Pâté (top) and Salmon Terrine (bottom).

This page: Garlic Shrimp and Mushrooms. Facing page: Paprika Shrimp (top) and Calamares España (bottom).

Separate heads of the squid from the tails. Remove the ink-sac and reserve for the sauce if desired. Remove the quill and discard. Cut the tentacles above the eyes, and reserve. Discard the eyes and head. Peel the purplish membrane off the tail portion of the squid. Split the tail in half, length-wise, and wash it well. Cut the tail into pieces about 2″ wide. Score each section in a lattice pattern at ¼″ intervals. Separate the tentacles. Put the squid, bay leaf and onion into a casserole with hot water. Cover loosely and cook for 1 minute on HIGH. Heat the olive oil for 30 seconds on HIGH in a medium-sized bowl. Add the garlic and onion, and cook for a further 1 minute on HIGH. Stir in the flour. Mix the cooking liquid from the squid with the tomatoes and the other sauce ingredients. If using the ink, break the ink-sac into the sauce ingredients. Cook the sauce, uncovered, for 5 minutes on HIGH. Mix with the squid and serve garnished with fresh coriander leaves.

Garlic Shrimp and Mushrooms

PREPARATION TIME: 10 minutes	
MICROWAVE COOKING TIME: 3-4 minutes	
SERVES: 4 people	

4-8 (depending on size) oyster or wild
   mushrooms
½ cup butter
1½ lbs raw shrimp, peeled
1 large clove garlic, chopped
2 tbsps chopped parsley
Salt and pepper
Lemon juice

Leave the mushrooms whole, but remove the stalks. Melt the butter in a shallow casserole for 30 seconds on HIGH. Add the mushrooms, garlic, salt, pepper and lemon juice. Cook for 2 minutes on HIGH. Remove and set aside. Add the shrimp to the casserole and cook on HIGH for 1 minute, stirring several times. Cook for 30 seconds more on HIGH, if required, to cook the shrimp thoroughly. Mix in the parsley and add more seasoning if necessary. Arrange the mushrooms in individual dishes and spoon over the shrimp and any remaining butter in the dish. Serve with French bread.

Microwave
FISH AND SEAFOOD

LIGHT DISHES

Codfish Pie

PREPARATION TIME: 15 minutes

MICROWAVE COOKING TIME: 11-12 minutes

SERVES: 4 people

4 cod fillets
2 tbsps lemon juice
2 tbsps water
1 bay leaf

SAUCE
3 tbsps butter
1 shallot, finely chopped
3 tbsps flour
1½ cups milk
2 tbsps chopped parsley
Salt and pepper

TOPPING
*2 large potatoes, peeled and very thinly
   sliced*
¼ cup grated Colby cheese
Paprika

Put the fillets in a casserole with the
water, lemon juice and bay leaf.
Cover loosely and cook for 2
minutes on HIGH. Melt the butter in
a deep bowl for 30 seconds on
HIGH. Add the shallot and cook for
a further 1 minute on HIGH. Stir in
the flour, milk, liquid from the fish,
salt, pepper and parsley. Cook for
2-3 minutes on HIGH or until thick,
stirring frequently. Pour over the cod.
Slice the potatoes on a mandolin or
with the fine blade of a food
processor. Layer on top of the cod

**This page: Codfish Pie (top) and
Tuna, Pea and Fennel Casserole
(bottom). Facing page: Sea Lion.**

and season with salt and pepper. Cover the dish tightly and cook for 3 minutes on HIGH. Sprinkle on the cheese and paprika and cook, uncovered, for a further 2 minutes on MEDIUM to melt the cheese. Serve immediately.

Crab Lasagne

PREPARATION TIME: 15 minutes

MICROWAVE COOKING TIME: 10 minutes

SERVES: 4 people

8 quick-cooking green lasagne noodles
4 tomatoes, peeled and sliced
8oz crabmeat, flaked
12oz Ricotta cheese
¼ cup grated Parmesan cheese
½ cup milk
1 small clove garlic, minced
Pinch marjoram
Pinch nutmeg
Pinch dry mustard
Salt and pepper

TOPPING
¼ cup seasoned dry breadcrumbs
1 tbsp butter
Paprika

Boil 3½ cups water on HIGH with a pinch of salt. Put in the lasagne and leave for 1 minute. Remove the noodles and rinse under hot water. Dry on paper towels. Mix the remaining ingredients, except the tomatoes, together. If the mixture is very thick, add more milk. Layer up the noodles, tomatoes and crabmeat filling, ending with filling. Melt the butter on HIGH for 30 seconds and stir in the breadcrumbs. Scatter over the top of the lasagne and sprinkle on some paprika. Cook for 3 minutes on HIGH and serve immediately.

Sea Lion

PREPARATION TIME: 20 minutes

MICROWAVE COOKING TIME: 5 minutes

SERVES: 4 people

CRABMEAT BALLS
1lb crabmeat, flaked
3 tbsps sherry
1 tbsp soy sauce
4 water chestnuts, finely chopped
2 green onions, finely chopped
2 tbsps cornstarch
1 egg white, lightly beaten
Pinch ginger
Salt and pepper

ACCOMPANIMENT
1 head Chinese cabbage, shredded
1 tbsp cornstarch
2 tbsps soy sauce
1 tsp sugar
½ cup chicken stock

GARNISH
Sesame seeds

Mix all the ingredients for the crabmeat balls together and shape into 2″ balls. Place them in a large casserole with 2 tbsps water. Cover loosely and cook for 2 minutes on MEDIUM. Remove from the casserole and keep warm. Combine the ingredients for the accompaniment and cook in the casserole for 2 minutes on HIGH, or until the cornstarch thickens. Put the crabmeat balls on top of the cabbage and heat through for 1 minute on HIGH. Sprinkle over the sesame seeds to serve.

Monkfish Provençale

PREPARATION TIME: 20 minutes

MICROWAVE COOKING TIME: 19 minutes

SERVES: 4 people

1½ lbs monkfish tails
1 eggplant, cut in ½″ chunks
2 zucchini, cut in ½″ chunks
1 large red pepper, cut in thin strips
¾ cup sliced mushrooms
1 large onion, thinly sliced
2 tbsps olive oil
1 clove garlic, crushed
½ cup white wine
7oz can plum tomatoes
2 tbsps tomato paste
Pinch dried thyme

1 bay leaf
Salt and pepper
½ cup grated cheese

Cut the eggplant in half lengthwise and lightly score the surface. Sprinkle with salt and leave to stand for 30 minutes. Wash and pat dry before cutting in cubes. Heat the olive oil in a browning dish for 3 minutes on HIGH. Add the vegetables and garlic. Cook for 2 minutes on HIGH. Add the canned tomatoes, tomato paste, thyme, bay leaf, half the wine, salt and pepper. Pour the contents into a casserole dish, cover, and cook for 10 minutes on HIGH. Stir 3 or 4 times during cooking. Cook the fish separately in the remaining wine for 2 minutes on HIGH. Transfer the fish to a baking dish and cover with the Provençale vegetables. Sprinkle on the cheese and cook for 2 minutes on MEDIUM to melt.

Tuna, Pea and Fennel Casserole

PREPARATION TIME: 15 minutes

MICROWAVE COOKING TIME: 10 minutes, plus 10 minutes standing time

SERVES: 4 people

8oz green and whole-wheat noodles
1 cup frozen peas
1 small bulb Florentine fennel chopped
8oz can tuna, drained
3 tbsps butter or margarine
3 tbsps flour
¼ cup white wine
1¼ cups milk
Pinch oregano
1 small clove garlic, minced
Salt and pepper

TOPPING
Paprika
Parmesan cheese

Facing page: Monkfish Provençale (top) and Crab Lasagne (bottom).

Put the noodles in a large bowl with 3½ cups water. Cook for 6 minutes on HIGH and then leave to stand for 10 minutes. Drain, rinse under hot water, then leave to dry. Put the fennel into a casserole with 2 tbsps water. Cover and cook for 1 minute on HIGH. Drain and combine with the noodles, tuna and peas. Melt the butter for 30 seconds on HIGH with the garlic. Stir in the flour, wine, milk, oregano, salt and pepper. Pour over the noodles and mix well. Sprinkle on grated Parmesan cheese and paprika. Heat for 2 minutes on HIGH before serving.

Shrimp Curry

PREPARATION TIME: 10 minutes

MICROWAVE COOKING TIME: 5-7 minutes

SERVES: 4 people

3 tbsps butter or margarine
3 tbsps flour
1 small onion, finely chopped
1 tbsp curry powder
1½ cups milk
¼ cup plain yogurt
1 cap pimento, chopped
8oz shrimp, cooked and peeled

This page: Seafood Stir-fry. Facing page: Shrimp Curry (top) and Pasta alla Vongole (bottom).

Desiccated coconut or chopped green onion

Melt the butter for 30 seconds on HIGH. Add the onion and cook for 30 seconds on HIGH to soften. Stir in the curry powder and cook for 1 minute on HIGH. Add the flour, salt, pepper and milk. Cook for 3-4 minutes, stirring often until thickened. Add the yogurt, pimento and shrimp. Heat for 30 seconds on HIGH and serve on a bed of rice. Sprinkle on the coconut or onion.

Seafood Stir-fry

PREPARATION TIME: 20 minutes

MICROWAVE COOKING TIME: 16 minutes

SERVES: 4 people

4oz thin Chinese egg noodles
2 tbsps vegetable oil
2 large or 4 small scallops
½ cup crabmeat, flaked
½ cup shrimp, cooked and peeled
4 water chestnuts, sliced
4 ears baby corn
2oz peapods
1 small red pepper, sliced
8oz bean sprouts
½ cup chicken or fish stock
2 tbsps soy sauce
1 tbsp cornstarch
1 tbsp sherry
Dash sesame seed oil
Salt and pepper

Boil 3½ cups water with a pinch of salt for 5 minutes on HIGH. Put in the noodles and leave them to stand for 6 minutes. Drain and rinse under hot water and leave to dry. Heat the oil for 5 minutes on HIGH in a browning dish. Cook the scallops for 3 minutes on HIGH, turning several times. Add the pepper, peapods and baby corn. Cook for 1 minute on HIGH. Add the bean sprouts and noodles. Mix the remaining ingredients together and add to the dish with the shrimp and crab. Toss the ingredients together and heat for 2 minutes on HIGH or until the sauce thickens. Serve immediately.

Pasta alla Vongole

PREPARATION TIME: 15 minutes

MICROWAVE COOKING TIME: 9 minutes, plus 10 minutes standing time

SERVES: 4 people

2 cups red, green and plain pasta shells (or other shapes)

3 tomatoes, peeled, seeded and sliced in strips
3 tbsps butter or margarine
½ clove garlic, crushed
2 shallots, finely chopped
3 tbsps flour
½ cup white wine
1 cup milk, or light cream
1 tbsp chopped parsley
Pinch oregano or basil
1½ cups small clams, shelled
Salt and pepper
Grated Parmesan cheese

Put the pasta into 3½ cups hot water with a pinch of salt. Cook for 6 minutes on HIGH. Leave to stand for 10 minutes, then drain and rinse in hot water. Melt the butter in a small, deep bowl for 30 seconds on HIGH. Add the garlic and shallot and cook for 30 seconds on HIGH to soften. Stir in the flour, wine and milk or cream, and add the herbs, salt and pepper. Cook for 2-3 minutes on HIGH, stirring every 30 seconds. Cut the tomatoes into thin strips and add to the hot sauce with the clams. Heat through for a further 30 seconds on HIGH. Toss the sauce and pasta together and serve with grated Parmesan cheese if desired.

MAIN DISHES

Turbot with Almonds and Emerald Sauce

PREPARATION TIME: 20 minutes

MICROWAVE COOKING TIME:
11 minutes

SERVES: 4 people

4 turbot fillets
1 slice onion
1 bay leaf
2 black peppercorns
½ cup water

SAUCE
1lb fresh spinach, well washed
1 tbsp fresh chives, chopped
1 tbsp white wine vinegar
Nutmeg
Cayenne pepper
1 tbsp butter
½ cup cream

GARNISH
½ cup sliced almonds

Heat a browning dish for 5 minutes on HIGH and toast the almonds for 1-2 minutes on HIGH, stirring frequently until browned. Put the fish into a casserole with the slice of onion, bay leaf, peppercorn, lemon juice and water. Cover loosely and cook on HIGH for 2 minutes. Set aside. Put the spinach, nutmeg, Cayenne pepper and butter into a large bowl with 1 tbsp water. Cover loosely and cook on HIGH for 2 minutes. Purée in a food processor.

This page: Salmon and Broccoli Fricassee. Facing page: Turbot with Almonds and Emerald Sauce.

Add the cream, chives and some of the fish cooking liquid if the sauce is too thick. Sprinkle the toasted almonds on the fish and serve with the emerald sauce.

Garlic-Braised Tuna Steaks

PREPARATION TIME: 20 minutes

MICROWAVE COOKING TIME: 11-12 minutes

SERVES: 4 people

4 tuna steaks, cut 1" thick
1 clove garlic, peeled and cut in thin slivers
8oz button or pickling onions, peeled
1 tbsp butter
½ cup red wine
½ cup water
1 bay leaf

SAUCE
Cooking liquid from the fish
1 tbsp butter or margarine
1 tbsp flour
1 tbsp tomato paste
½ tsp thyme
1 tbsp chopped parsley
Squeeze lemon juice
Salt and pepper

GARNISH
1lb fresh spinach, washed and thinly shredded
1 tbsp butter

Make small slits in the tuna steaks with a knife and insert a sliver of garlic into each slit. Heat a browning dish for 3 minutes on HIGH. Drop in 1 tbsp butter and the peeled onions. Heat for 1-2 minutes on HIGH, stirring occasionally, until the onions begin to brown. Pour in the water and wine. Transfer the contents of the browning dish to a large casserole. Add the bay leaf and fish to the casserole, cover loosely and cook for 5 minutes on HIGH. Remove the fish and onions from the casserole and keep them warm. Melt 1 tbsp butter in a small, deep bowl for 30 seconds on HIGH. Stir in the flour and cook for 1-2 minutes on HIGH or until the flour is lightly browned. Pour in the cooking liquid

from the fish, and add the tomato paste and thyme. Cook for 2-3 minutes on HIGH, stirring occasionally until thickened. Add the parsley, lemon juice, salt and pepper, and set aside with the fish. Melt the remaining butter in a small casserole on HIGH for 30 seconds. Put in the spinach, cover loosely and cook for 1-2 minutes on HIGH. Spread the spinach onto a serving plate and combine the fish and sauce to re-heat for 30 seconds on HIGH. Arrange the fish and onions on top of the bed of spinach and pour over the sauce to serve.

Salmon and Broccoli Fricassee

PREPARATION TIME: 20 minutes

MICROWAVE COOKING TIME: 10-12 minutes

SERVES: 4 people

2lbs salmon fillets or tail pieces
½ cup sliced almonds, toasted
1lb broccoli
½ cup white wine
1 cup sliced mushrooms
1 tbsp butter
1 tbsp flour
1 cup chow mein noodles
1 tsp chopped dill
1 tsp chopped parsley
¾ cup cream
Salt and pepper

Put the fillets into a casserole with enough water to barely cover. Cover the dish loosely and cook for 2 minutes on HIGH. Reserve the cooking liquid, flake the fish and set aside. Put the broccoli into a bowl with 2 tbsps water. Cover loosely and cook for 4 minutes on HIGH. Drain and arrange the broccoli in a casserole with the flaked salmon. Melt the butter in a small bowl for 30 seconds on HIGH. Stir in the flour, cream, fish liquid and sliced mushrooms. Cook for 2-3 minutes on HIGH. Season with salt and pepper. Add dill and parsley and pour over the fish and broccoli. Sprinkle over the almonds and

noodles. Heat through for 2 minutes on HIGH before serving.

Halibut à la Normande

PREPARATION TIME: 15 minutes

MICROWAVE COOKING TIME: 5-7 minutes

SERVES: 4 people

4 halibut fillets or steaks
½ cup white wine, dry cider or unsweetened apple juice
¼ cup water
1 tbsp flour
2 tbsps butter or margarine
1 shallot, finely chopped
2 medium-sized apples
¼ cup light cream
1 bay leaf
Salt and pepper
Lemon juice

GARNISH
Chopped parsley

Put the halibut into a casserole with the wine, cider or juice, water and bay leaf. Cover loosely and cook for 2 minutes on HIGH. Set aside and keep warm. In a small bowl melt half the butter. Add the shallot and cook, uncovered, for 1 minute on HIGH, stirring once. Peel and chop one of the apples. Add the shallot, cover the bowl loosely and cook for 2 minutes on HIGH, or until the apple is soft. Stir in the flour, add the cooking liquid from the fish and heat for 2 minutes on HIGH. Stir the sauce twice until thickened. Add the cream and heat for 30 seconds on HIGH. Season with salt, pepper and lemon juice to taste. Heat a browning dish for 5 minutes on HIGH and drop in the remaining butter. Core and slice the second apple, but do not peel it. Brown the slices for 1-2 minutes on HIGH in the butter. Coat the fish with the sauce and garnish with the parsley. Serve surrounded with the apple slices.

Facing page: Garlic-Braised Tuna Steaks.

Monkfish Medallions Piperade

PREPARATION TIME: 15 minutes

MICROWAVE COOKING TIME: 7 minutes, plus 1 minute standing time

SERVES: 4 people

2lbs monkfish tails
½ cup white wine
1½ cups tomato sauce
1 shallot, finely chopped
1 red pepper, sliced
1 green pepper, sliced
1 yellow pepper, sliced
1 clove garlic, finely minced
½ tsp thyme
1 bay leaf
Salt and pepper

GARNISH
Chopped parsley

Cut the monkfish tails into round slices ½″ thick. Put into a casserole with the wine and bay leaf. Cover loosely and cook for 2 minutes on HIGH. Set aside. Combine the shallot, garlic and thyme in a small, deep bowl. Pour on the fish cooking liquid and cook, uncovered, for 3 minutes on HIGH to reduce by half. Add the tomato sauce, peppers, salt and pepper. Cover loosely and cook for 2 minutes on HIGH. Leave to stand for 1 minute and pour over the fish to serve.

Salmon in Chive Sauce

PREPARATION TIME: 15 minutes

MICROWAVE COOKING TIME: 5 minutes

SERVES: 4 people

1 side of salmon (about 1½-2lbs)
2 tbsps butter or margarine
1 cup sour cream
½ cup light cream
1 tsp cornstarch
3 tbsps snipped chives
1 tsp coarsely ground black pepper
Salt

Slice the salmon horizontally into very thin slices. Heat a browning dish for 3 minutes on HIGH. Drop in the butter and heat for 30 seconds on HIGH. Lay in the salmon slices and cook for 30 seconds each side. Cook the fish in several batches. Remove the fish from the dish. Cover and keep warm. Mix the cream, sour cream, and cornstarch together. Pour into the dish and cook for 30 seconds on HIGH. Stir well and repeat the process until the cornstarch has cooked and thickened

This page: Monkfish Medallions Piperade. Facing page: Halibut à la Normande (top) and Salmon in Chive Sauce (bottom).

the sauce. The sauce should not bubble too rapidly, but the cornstarch will help prevent the sour cream from curdling. Stir in the chives, pepper and salt, and pour over the salmon slices. Serve with fine green noodles.

Sole in Lettuce Leaf Parcels

PREPARATION TIME: 20 minutes

MICROWAVE COOKING TIME:
5 minutes

SERVES: 4 people

4 double fillets of sole or flounder
8 large leaves of romaine lettuce
8oz small shrimp
1 finely chopped shallot
½ cup chopped mushrooms
2 tbsps chopped parsley
4 large caps canned pimento
1 cap pimento, chopped
½ cup white wine
½ cup heavy cream
1 cup low-fat soft cheese
Salt and pepper

Combine the shrimp, mushrooms, half the parsley, salt and pepper, and stuff the pimento caps with the mixture. Roll the fish fillets around the pimento and set aside. Put the lettuce leaves into a large casserole with 2 tbsps water. Cover tightly and cook for 30 seconds on HIGH to

This page: Sole in Lettuce Leaf Parcels. Facing page: Mackerel and Mustard (top) and Trout with Hazelnuts (bottom).

soften. Roll the leaves carefully around the stuffed fillets. Put seam-side down into a casserole with the wine and shallot. Cover loosely and cook for 3 minutes on HIGH. Remove the parcels and keep them warm. Cook the wine for a further 2-3 minutes on HIGH to reduce. Stir

in the cream and bring to the boil for 2 minutes on HIGH. Add the cheese, salt, pepper, the remaining parsley and chopped pimento. Serve the sauce with the sole parcels.

Trout with Hazelnuts

PREPARATION TIME: 15 minutes

MICROWAVE COOKING TIME: 12-13 minutes

SERVES: 4 people

4 small rainbow trout, cleaned
4 tbsps butter
¾ cup crushed hazelnuts
4 green onions, shredded
Juice of 1 lemon
Salt and pepper

Heat a browning dish for 5 minutes on HIGH. Put in the hazelnuts and cook for 2-3 minutes on HIGH, stirring often until browned. Set aside. Melt half the butter in the browning dish. Add the trout and cook for 5 minutes per side. If the butter has browned too much, wipe out the dish. Melt the remaining butter and allow to brown lightly. Add the nuts, lemon juice and green onion, and season with salt and pepper. Pour over the fish to serve.

Hangchow Fish

PREPARATION TIME: 15 minutes

MICROWAVE COOKING TIME: 19 minutes

SERVES: 4 people

1 sea or freshwater bass, 2-2¼ lbs in
    weight, cleaned
½ cup white wine
½ cup water
1 small ginger root, sliced
¼ cup sugar
⅓ cup rice vinegar
2 tbsps soy sauce
1 tbsp cornstarch
1 clove garlic, minced
1 carrot, thinly sliced in rounds
4 water chestnuts, thinly sliced

4 green onions, diagonally sliced
Salt and pepper

Combine the wine, water and a few slices of ginger in a large casserole. Cut 2 or 3 slashes on each side of the fish to help it cook faster, and put it into the casserole. Cover and cook for 25 minutes on MEDIUM. Set the fish aside and keep it warm. Combine the cornstarch, sugar, vinegar, soy sauce, salt, pepper and ½ cup of the fish cooking liquid. Add the garlic and cook on HIGH for 2 minutes, stirring frequently. Add the water chestnuts, carrots and remaining slices of ginger. Cook the sauce for a further 1-2 minutes on HIGH. Add the green onions and pour over the fish to serve.

Mackerel and Mustard

PREPARATION TIME: 15 minutes

MICROWAVE COOKING TIME: 14-16 minutes

SERVES: 4 people

4 small mackerel, cleaned
1 cup white wine
1 tsp whole mustard seed
3 whole peppercorns
1 bay leaf
1 slice onion

SAUCE
1½ tbsps flour
1½ tbsps butter
2 tbsps Dijon or spicy brown mustard
2 tbsps chopped herbs (eg chives, parsley,
    thyme, dill)
½ cup milk
Salt and pepper

Put the mackerel into one or two casseroles (do not crowd the fish) and cook in two batches if necessary. Pour over the white wine and add the mustard seed, peppercorns, bay leaf and onion. Cover loosely and cook for 12 minutes on HIGH. Set aside and keep warm. Melt the butter in a small, deep bowl for 30 seconds on HIGH. Stir in the flour, milk and strained liquid from the fish. Cook, uncovered, for 2-3 minutes on

HIGH, stirring often until thickened. Add salt, pepper, mustard and herbs. Peel the skin from one side of the mackerel and coat each one with some of the sauce to serve. Serve the remaining sauce separately.

Crab-Stuffed Trout

PREPARATION TIME: 15 minutes

MICROWAVE COOKING TIME: 14 minutes

SERVES: 4 people

4 rainbow trout
4 tbsps butter
Juice of 1 lemon

STUFFING
8oz flaked crabmeat
3 green onions, chopped
2 sticks celery, finely chopped
1 small green pepper, finely chopped
¼ cup black olives, sliced
Fresh breadcrumbs from 4 slices of white
    bread, crusts removed
2 tbsps chopped parsley
2 tbsps sherry
Salt and pepper

GARNISH
Lemon slices
Chopped chives

Buy the trout fresh or frozen with the bones removed. Mix the stuffing ingredients together and fill the trout. Put the trout into a large casserole and cook, covered, in two batches if necessary. Cook 4 trout together for 12 minutes on HIGH, or 2 trout for 6 minutes on HIGH. Melt the butter for 2 minutes on HIGH and add the lemon juice and pour over the trout before serving. Garnish with lemon slices and chives.

Facing page: Hangchow Fish.

Sole and Asparagus Rolls

PREPARATION TIME: 15 minutes

MICROWAVE COOKING TIME:
7 minutes

SERVES: 4 people

8 fillets of sole
16 asparagus spears
½ cup water
1 tbsp lemon juice

SAUCE
3 egg yolks
2 tbsps lemon juice
½ cup butter
Cayenne pepper
Salt

**This page: Sole and Asparagus
Rolls. Facing page: Crab-Stuffed
Trout.**

Cook the asparagus with 2 tbsps
water for 2 minutes on HIGH in a
covered casserole. Rinse under cold
water and drain dry. Divide the
asparagus evenly between all the sole
fillets and roll the fish around them.
Tuck the ends of the fillets under the
asparagus evenly between all the sole
fillets and roll the fish around them.
Tuck the ends of the fillets under the
asparagus and place in a casserole.

Pour over the water and 1 tbsp lemon juice. Cover the dish loosely and cook for 2-3 minutes on HIGH. Set aside and keep warm. Melt the butter in a small, deep bowl for 1 minute on HIGH. Beat the egg yolks, lemon juice, salt and Cayenne pepper together. Have a bowl of iced water ready. Pour the yolk mixture into the butter and beat well. Cook for 30 seconds on HIGH and beat well. Repeat the process until the sauce thickens – about 2 minutes. Put the sauce bowl into the iced water to stop the cooking. Pour over the hot fish and asparagus rolls to serve. Sprinkle on paprika if desired.

Sole with Limes and Chili Peppers

PREPARATION TIME: 15 minutes

MICROWAVE COOKING TIME:
6 minutes

SERVES: 4 people

2lbs sole fillets
2 limes
1 green chili pepper, very thinly sliced
1 small bunch chives
2 tbsps butter
Salt and pepper

Melt the butter in a large casserole for 1 minute on HIGH. Put in the fish and cook for 30 seconds each side on HIGH. Remove from the casserole and keep warm. Grate the peel off one of the limes, pare off the white pith and cut the lime into very thin rounds. Squeeze the remaining lime for its juice. Pour the lime juice into the casserole with the butter. Add the chili pepper slices and cook for 30 seconds on HIGH. Add the lime slices, rind and snipped chives. Season and pour over the fish fillets to serve.

Salmon with Tomato Chive Hollandaise

PREPARATION TIME: 15 minutes

MICROWAVE COOKING TIME:
4 minutes

SERVES: 4 people

4 salmon fillets or tail portions
2 tomatoes, peeled, seeded and chopped
2 tbsps snipped chives
3 egg yolks
½ cup butter
1 tsp red wine vinegar
Salt and pepper

Poach the fish fillets in enough water to come half way up the side of the fillets. Cover loosely and cook for 2 minutes on HIGH. Keep warm. Beat the yolks with salt, pepper and chives. Add the vinegar and set aside. Melt the butter for 1 minute on HIGH in a small, deep bowl. Beat the yolks into the butter. Have a bowl of iced water ready. Put the sauce ingredients into the oven and cook for 20 seconds on HIGH. Stir and cook for 20 seconds more. Repeat until the sauce thickens – about 2 minutes. Put the bowl into the iced water to stop the cooking process. Add the tomatoes to the sauce and serve with the salmon fillets.

Sole Bonne Femme

PREPARATION TIME: 20 minutes

MICROWAVE COOKING TIME:
8-11 minutes

SERVES: 4 people

2lbs sole fillets
8oz whole mushrooms, stalks removed
4oz button or pickling onions, peeled
½ cup white wine
1 bay leaf

WHITE SAUCE
2 tbsps butter or margarine
2 tbsps flour
½ cup milk
Salt and pepper

BUTTER SAUCE
2 egg yolks
¼ cup butter
½ tbsp white wine vinegar
Salt and pepper

For the butter sauce, melt ¼ cup butter in a small, deep bowl for 30 seconds on HIGH. Mix the egg yolks, vinegar, salt and pepper together and beat into the butter. Have a bowl of iced water ready. Cook the sauce for 15 seconds on HIGH and beat well. Repeat until the sauce has thickened – about 1 minute. Put immediately into a bowl of iced water to stop the cooking. Set the sauce aside. Tuck the ends of each sole fillet under and place the fish into a large casserole. Add the mushrooms, onions, wine and bay leaf. Cover loosely and cook for 5-6 minutes on HIGH. Arrange the fish, mushrooms and onions in a clean casserole or serving dish and keep warm. In a small bowl melt the remaining butter on HIGH for 30 seconds. Stir in the flour, milk, cooking liquid from the fish, salt and pepper. Cook for 2-3 minutes on HIGH, stirring frequently until thickened. Beat in the butter sauce and pour over the fish to serve.

Cod with Bacon

PREPARATION TIME: 15 minutes

MICROWAVE COOKING TIME:
12 minutes

SERVES: 4 people

4 fillets of cod
¼ cup white wine
8 strips bacon, rind and bones removed
1 green pepper, diced
2 green onions, chopped
1 tbsp flour
½ cup milk
1 bay leaf
Salt and pepper

Put the cod, wine and bay leaf into a large casserole. Cover loosely and cook on HIGH for 3 minutes. Set aside. Heat a browning dish for 3 minutes on HIGH. Chop the bacon roughly, put it into the browning dish

Facing page: Sole Bonne Femme (top) and Salmon with Tomato Chive Hollandaise (bottom).

and cook for 2-3 minutes on HIGH. Stir frequently until the bacon has browned. Add the pepper and onion and cook for 30 seconds on HIGH. Stir in the flour, milk, salt, pepper and liquid from the fish. Cook for 2-3 minutes on HIGH, stirring frequently until the sauce has thickened. Pour over the fish and re-heat for 30 seconds on HIGH. Serve with parsley new potatoes.

Sole with Oranges

PREPARATION TIME: 15 minutes

MICROWAVE COOKING TIME: 5 minutes

SERVES: 4 people

2lbs sole fillets
¾ cup orange juice
1 tbsp lemon juice
2 tsps butter
2 tsps flour
¾ cup heavy cream
1 tbsp chopped basil
Salt and pepper

GARNISH
2 oranges, peeled and cut in segments
Fresh basil leaves, if available

Tuck in the ends of the sole fillets. Put into a casserole with the orange and lemon juice. Cover loosely and cook on HIGH for 2 minutes. Set aside. Melt the butter in a small, deep bowl for 30 seconds on HIGH. Add the flour and fish cooking liquid. Stir in the cream, basil, salt and pepper, and cook, uncovered, for 2 minutes on HIGH. Stir frequently until the sauce thickens. Pour over the fish and serve with the orange segments and basil leaves.

Cod with Crumb Topping

PREPARATION TIME: 10 minutes

MICROWAVE COOKING TIME: 5-7 minutes

SERVES: 4 people

4 cod fillets
Lemon juice
½ cup water

TOPPING
4 tbsps butter or margarine
1½ cups seasoned breadcrumbs
2 tbsp paprika
¼ cup grated Parmesan cheese
2 tbsps sesame seeds
Salt and pepper

GARNISH
Lemon wedges

Heat a browning dish for 3 minutes on HIGH. Melt the butter in the dish and add the breadcrumbs. Stir well and heat for 1 minute on HIGH to lightly brown. Add the remaining

This page: Cod with Crumb Topping (top) and Cod with Bacon (bottom). Facing page: Sole with Limes and Chili Peppers (top) and Sole with Oranges (bottom).

ingredients and heat for 1 minute more on HIGH. Set aside. Put the cod, a squeeze of lemon juice, and water into a casserole. Cover loosely and cook for 3-4 minutes on HIGH. Drain the fillets and top each one with the breadcrumb mixture. Heat through for 30 seconds on HIGH. Serve with lemon wedges.

Lychee Sole

PREPARATION TIME: 20 minutes

MICROWAVE COOKING TIME:
4-5 minutes

SERVES: 4 people

2lbs sole fillets
8oz lychees (canned or fresh), peeled
8oz can pineapple chunks, ½ cup juice
  reserved
Juice and rind of 2 limes
1-2 tbsps sugar
1 tbsp light soy sauce
2 tsps cornstarch

2 green onions, shredded
Salt and pepper

With a swivel peeler, peel strips off
the limes, and cut into thin slivers.
Cover well and set aside. Squeeze the
lime juice, and mix with the
pineapple juice, sugar, soy sauce and
constarch in a small, deep bowl. Fold
the fish fillets in half and place in a
large casserole, thinner ends of the
fillets towards the middle of the dish.
Pour over enough water to cover ½″
of the sides of the fillets. Cover the
dish loosely and cook for 2 minutes
on HIGH. Set aside and keep warm.

**This page: Lychee Sole. Facing
page: Sole Italienne (top) and
Halibut and Green Grapes
(bottom).**

Cook the sauce ingredients for 2-3
minutes on HIGH, stirring often
until thickened. Add the cooking
liquid from the fish, strained. Stir in
the pineapple chunks, lychees, green
onions and lime rind. Add a pinch of
salt and pepper and pour the sauce
over the fish. Serve with fried rice or
chow mein noodles.

Halibut and Green Grapes

PREPARATION TIME: 10 minutes

MICROWAVE COOKING TIME: 10-13 minutes

SERVES: 4 people

2lbs halibut steaks
1 small bunch green seedless grapes
½ cup white wine
Lemon juice
¾ cup heavy cream
1 tsp tarragon
Salt and pepper

Put the fish into a casserole and pour on the wine and lemon juice. Cook for 4-5 minutes on HIGH. Remove the fish from the casserole, cover and keep warm. Heat the wine for 2-3 minutes on HIGH to reduce by half. Cut the grapes in half if large, and add to the wine. Add the tarragon, salt and pepper, and cream. Heat through for 1 minute on HIGH. Pour over the fish to serve.

Halibut in Sesame Ginger Sauce

PREPARATION TIME: 20 minutes

MICROWAVE COOKING TIME: 6 minutes

SERVES: 4 people

4 halibut steaks
2 carrots, cut in Julienne strips
1 cup water
3 tbsps ginger wine
¼ cup light brown sugar
¼ cup sesame seeds
2 tbsps chopped fresh ginger root
2 tbsps rice vinegar
2 tsps cornstarch
Dash of sesame seed oil
Salt and pepper

Put the fish into a casserole with the ginger wine and water. Cover and cook for 2 minutes on HIGH. Put the carrots into a small bowl with 1 tbsp water. Cover loosely and cook for 1 minute on HIGH. Leave to stand while preparing the sauce. Combine the sugar, cornstarch,

ginger, sesame seed oil, rice vinegar, sesame seeds and cooking liquid from the fish. Cook for 4 minutes on HIGH, stirring often until thickened. Add the carrot, salt and pepper and pour over the fish to serve.

Sole Italienne

PREPARATION TIME: 15 minutes

MICROWAVE COOKING TIME: 6-8 minutes

SERVES: 4 people

8 sole fillets
4oz Parma ham
½ cup white wine
1 tbsp butter or margarine
1 tbsp flour
¾ cup heavy cream
Pinch sage
Pinch thyme
Pinch chopped parsley
1 bay leaf
Salt and pepper

GARNISH
Fresh sage or bay leaves

Cut the ham into ½" strips. Wrap the ham strips lattice fashion around the fish and tuck the ends underneath. Put into a casserole with the bay leaf and wine. Cook for 3-4 minutes on HIGH. Remove the fish from the dish, cover and keep it warm. Discard the bay leaf. Melt the butter for 30 seconds on HIGH in a small casserole. Stir in the flour and fish cooking liquid, and add the thyme, parsley, sage, salt and pepper. Cook for 2 minutes on HIGH and stir in the cream. Cook for a further 1 minute on HIGH and spoon over the fish. Garnish with sage or bay leaves.

Fillets of Salmon with Peppercorn Sauce

PREPARATION TIME: 15 minutes

MICROWAVE COOKING TIME: 8-12 minutes

SERVES: 4 people

1 side of salmon, about 1½-2lbs
2 tbsps butter or margarine
1 cup heavy cream
⅓ cup dry vermouth
1 tbsp canned green peppercorns, rinsed and drained
Salt and pepper

Slice the salmon horizontally into very thin slices. Heat a browning dish for 3 minutes on HIGH. Drop in the butter and heat for 30 seconds on HIGH. Lay in the salmon slices and cook for 30 seconds each side. Cook the fish in several batches. Remove the cooked fish from the dish, cover it, and keep it warm. Pour the vermouth into the dish and add the peppercorns. Cook on HIGH for 2 minutes or until reduced by half. Add the cream, stir well, and cook for 2-3 minutes on HIGH until bubbling. Season with salt and pepper. Pour over the salmon scallops to serve. Serve with lightly cooked green beans or pea-pods.

Fruits of the Sea

PREPARATION TIME: 15 minutes

MICROWAVE COOKING TIME: 5-9 minutes

SERVES: 4 people

2lbs mixture of:
    raw scallops, cut in half
    raw shrimp, peeled
    1 lobster tail, shelled and cut into 1" chunks
    sole fillets, cut into 2" chunks
    oysters, shelled
    mussels, shelled
1 cup white wine
2 tsps cornstarch
1 tbsp lemon juice
½ cup whole-milk yogurt
2 tbsps chopped chives
8oz edible seaweed, soaked or cooked in 2 tbsps water
Salt and pepper

Facing page: Fruits of the Sea (top) and Fillets of Salmon with Peppercorn Sauce (bottom).

Cook all the seafood in the wine for 2-3 minutes on HIGH. Cook the seaweed with 2 tbsps water for 1-2 minutes on HIGH. Mix the cornstarch and lemon juice. Remove the fish from the casserole and arrange on a serving dish with the seaweed. Combine the cornstarch and lemon juice with the cooking liquid from the seafood. Cook for 2-3 minutes on HIGH, stirring frequently until thickened. Add the yogurt and chives and heat through for 30 seconds on HIGH. Season with salt and pepper and pour over the seafood.

Salmon in Madeira

PREPARATION TIME: 15 minutes

MICROWAVE COOKING TIME: 8 minutes

SERVES: 4 people

4 salmon steaks, about 1" thick
8oz mushrooms, stalks trimmed
5 sprigs fresh rosemary
1 cup Rainwater Madeira
½ cup water
1 tbsp butter or margarine
1 tbsp flour
Small pinch ground cloves
¼ cup heavy cream
Salt and pepper

Put the salmon steaks in a casserole with the Madeira. Strip the leaves off one sprig of rosemary and add to the salmon. Cover the dish loosely and cook for 5 minutes on HIGH. Add the mushrooms half way through the cooking time. Melt the butter in a small casserole for 2 minutes on HIGH until browning slightly. Add the flour and cook for 1 minute on HIGH. Stir in the cooking liquid from the fish and a pinch of cloves. Season with salt and pepper. Arrange the salmon and mushrooms on plates and pour over the Madeira sauce. Drizzle 1 tbsp cream over each salmon steak and garnish each with a sprig of fresh rosemary.

Curried Cod Nuggets

PREPARATION TIME: 15 minutes

MICROWAVE COOKING TIME: 7 minutes

SERVES: 4 people

2lbs cod, cut in 2" chunks
¼ cup lime juice
¾ cup water
2 tbsps butter or margarine
2 tbsps flour
1 large onion, chopped
1 tbsp curry powder
½ cup orange juice
2 oranges, peeled and segmented
2 tomatoes, peeled and seeded
Desiccated coconut

Combine the cod, lime juice and water in a large casserole. Cover loosely and cook on HIGH for 2 minutes. Set aside and keep warm. Melt the butter for 30 seconds on HIGH in a small, deep bowl. Add the

This page: Curried Cod Nuggets. Facing page: Halibut in Sesame Ginger Sauce (top) and Salmon in Madeira (bottom).

onion, cover loosely and cook for 1 minute on HIGH. Stir in the curry powder and cook for 1 minute on HIGH. Add the flour, orange juice and cooking liquid from the fish. Stir well and cook, uncovered, for 2-3 minutes. Stir often until the sauce is thick. Slice the tomatoes into thin strips and add to the sauce with the orange segments. Cook the sauce for 10 seconds on HIGH to heat the orange and tomato through. Pour the sauce over the cod nuggets and sprinkle with desiccated coconut.

Monkfish and Ribbons

PREPARATION TIME: 20 minutes

MICROWAVE COOKING TIME:
5-6 minutes

SERVES: 4 people

2lbs monkfish tails
½ cup white wine
2 carrots, peeled
2 zucchini, ends trimmed
1 large or 2 small leeks, washed and
    trimmed, retaining some green
½ cup heavy cream
2 tbsps chopped parsley
½ tsp ground oregano
1 bay leaf
Salt and pepper

Cut the monkfish tails into ½"
rounds. Put the pieces into a
casserole with the wine and bay leaf.
Cover loosely and cook for 2
minutes on HIGH. Set aside and
keep warm. With a swivel vegetable
peeler, pare thin ribbons of carrot and
zucchini. Cut the leeks in half
lengthwise and then into ½" strips.
Put the vegetables into a small
casserole with 1 tbsp water. Cover
loosely and cook for 1 minute on
HIGH. Set aside. Remove the fish
from the casserole and heat the wine
for 2-3 minutes on HIGH to reduce.
Pour in the cream, and add the
oregano, salt and pepper. Heat
through for 30 seconds on HIGH.
Pour the sauce over the fish and
sprinkle on the chopped parsley.
Surround with the vegetable ribbons
to serve.

Cod Steaks with Mushrooms

PREPARATION TIME: 15 minutes

MICROWAVE COOKING TIME:
5-7 minutes

SERVES: 4 people

4-8 cod steaks, depending on size
½ cup white wine
1 bay leaf
2 shallots, finely chopped
2 tbsps butter
1½ cups sliced mushrooms
1 tbsp flour
½ cup milk
1 tsp Worcestershire sauce
1 tsp chopped parsley
Salt and pepper

Put the cod and wine into a casserole
with the bay leaf and shallot. Cover
loosely and cook for 2 minutes on
HIGH. Leave covered and set aside.
Melt the butter in a small bowl for
30 seconds on HIGH. Add the
mushrooms. Cover loosely and cook
for 1 minute on HIGH to soften
slightly. Stir in the flour, milk and
Worcestershire sauce. Remove the
bay leaf from the fish and add the
fish cooking liquid to the sauce
ingredients. Cook, uncovered, for 2-3
minutes on HIGH, stirring often
until thickened. Add salt, pepper and
parsley. Pour over the cod to serve.

Sole Aurora

PREPARATION TIME: 15 minutes

MICROWAVE COOKING TIME:
6-7 minutes

SERVES: 4 people

2lbs sole fillets
½ cup white wine
1 bay leaf

SAUCE
2 tbsps butter or margarine
2 tbsps flour
1 cup milk
Rind and juice of 1 orange
1 tbsp tomato paste
Salt and pepper

GARNISH
4 tomatoes, peeled, seeded and cut into
    thin strips

Cook the fish with the wine and the
bay leaf for 3 minutes on HIGH in a
loosely covered casserole. Melt the
butter in a small, deep bowl for
30 seconds on HIGH. Add the flour,
milk, tomato paste, fish cooking

**Facing page: Monkfish and
Ribbons.**

liquid, salt and pepper. Cook for 2-3 minutes on HIGH, stirring frequently until thickened. Add the rind and juice of the orange and cook for 30 seconds more on HIGH. Pour the sauce over the fish and top with the tomato strips.

Sea Bass and Fennel

PREPARATION TIME: 15 minutes

MICROWAVE COOKING TIME: 23 minutes

SERVES: 4 people

1 sea bass, weighing 2-2¼ lbs, cleaned and trimmed

2 bulbs Florentine fennel
4 oranges
Juice of 1 lemon
1 tbsp anise liqueur
1½ cups whole-milk yogurt
Salt
Coarsely ground pepper

GARNISH
Samphire
Orange slices

Squeeze the juice from one of the oranges and slice the others. Sprinkle the inside of the bass with salt and put it into a large, shallow casserole. Pour over the orange juice and lemon juice, cover and cook for 20 minutes

This page: Sole Aurora (left) and Cod Steaks with Mushrooms (right). Facing page: Sea Bass and Fennel.

on HIGH. Carefully lift out the fish and keep it warm. Cook the fennel in 2 tbsps water for 2 minutes on HIGH and set aside. Stir the liqueur, pepper and yogurt into the fish cooking liquid and heat through for 30 seconds on HIGH. Do not let the sauce boil. Peel the skin from the fish if desired and pour over the sauce. Garnish with the samphire and orange slices to serve. Prepare with other varieties of large whole fish if desired.

INDEX